Wisdom from the Sea

James W. Evanow

DEDICATION

I would like to dedicate this book to all of the people that have and continue to believe in me and to all of the people in the world that continue to chase their dreams, in hopes that they may make the world a better place.

CONTENTS

ACKNOWLEDGMENTS

I would like to acknowledge Susan Woods for her inspiration and help in pre-editing some of the stories in this book. Thank you Paul Hoyt for your suggestion that I write some short stories about my at sea experiences that have helped to shape me into who I am as a person.

I cannot move forward without thanking my children for believing in me and I hope that you all continue to believe in yourselves and chase your dreams.

But most of all... thank you to my dad for introducing me to the beauty, the majesty and the adventure of the sea.

INTRODUCTION

"The man who is calm has his course in life clearly marked on his chart. His hand is ever on the helm. Storm, fog, night, tempest, danger, and hidden reefs ... he is prepared and ready for them.

He is made calm and serene by the realization that in these crises of his voyage he needs a clear mind and a cool head; and he knows that he has naught to do but to do each day the best he can each day by the light that he has; that He will never flinch nor falter for a moment; though he may have to tack and leave his course for a time, he will never drift. He will get back into the true channel, he will keep ever headed to toward his harbor.

When he will reach it, how he will reach it, matters not to him. He rests in calmness knowing the serene knowledge that he has done his best. If his best seems to be overcome or overruled, then he must still bow his head . . . in calmness.

No man knows the future of his life, the finality. God commits to man only new beginnings, new wisdom, and new days to use the best of his knowledge."

—William George Jordan, *The Majesty of Calmness*

William George Jordan left us valuable advice, both in the metaphors he used from the sea and with his experiential life. He was from the same era as Ernest Shackleton, over 100 years ago. Shackleton was an expedition leader who never let challenges stop him. When these men were alive, their values were different from those of the modern day. They stood for integrity and morality. They knew what it took to lead people and to instill those same solid values into others below them on the chain of command. Shackleton and Jordan knew that calmness is a key ingredient in emotional intelligence and leadership, as referenced in the excerpt above.

Much of what these men stood for, and demanded from others, was possible because they did not let social constructs or beliefs inhibit their decision-making. It is my opinion that we all can learn from their examples—we can continue to pass on the same messages, and be of solid fiber and moral character. We can be authentic leaders to those who are lost and looking for answers.

I have written this book, using sea stories as anecdotes, in order to bring awareness about how we think and act, who we are, how we treat others. I touch on topics including emotional intelligence and leadership. This book also addresses change and its effect on us, risk-based decisions that can spell either failure or success, and the importance of working as a team and eliminating ego from the workplace.

I believe that we must continue to examine what we consider to be the reality of our lives. Why do we continue to do what we do? How much does the media sway us in what we believe to be true? I question our political leaders and hope to create awareness around what they are telling us is good for us.

It is my opinion that we need to continue to create awareness about how we are treating one another, and of how many people are struggling in the world who need to be encouraged.

We all want basically the same things in life. We want to be happy, to have freedom, and to be able to pursue our dreams. Many people just want to get along with others, and they want to see their children grow up in a safe environment. They want to be able to retire and to not have to worry about surviving the next day. However, for many, these basic dreams are not always fulfilled. Times are uncertain, and I believe that people are beginning to appreciate the simple things in life.

It is great to be able to have an abundance of material wealth, but there is so much more to life. This is what many of the spiritual teachers throughout history have taught us. Although it is positive to make money and to be financially secure, there is a point where financial greed will cloud our decision-making process and control our every move. This book is not meant to be provocative, but if it jars your belief patterns and you disagree with any points I make, I encourage you to think deeply about your beliefs. Ask yourself these questions: Who taught you that belief, or where did you hear it? When did they teach you, or how long ago was it? Things change with time, and so do we.

The sea is a great place for reflection. There is nowhere else on this planet where you can witness the severity of a storm, being pounded into oblivion, only to see the storm subside and then witness the calm as it gently takes over the elements. The metaphors of the sea are endless; if we can master this calmness when the storms of our lives overtake us, we will be able to master just about anything that comes our way.

We all have a responsibility to be an example to those around us, to be beacons of hope. We need leaders who will seek out those who are bewildered, and who will lift up the disenfran-chised. It is up to us to make a difference in our work place, our homes, and the world.

We have been told many things in our lives, and we have the choice to either believe what we are told, or to use our own minds and develop our own thoughts and opinions. It is a choice. No matter what you decide to do, I hope that this book will teach you to believe in one thing more than anything else—believe in yourself and believe that you can do anything you set your mind to, gracefully, with an open and compas-sionate heart.

I hope that you enjoy the stories and that you walk away with some of the wisdom that I have learned over the years. I hope that this book will help you to reflect upon your own life and help you to realize just how much opportunity and potential you have to succeed and be the best that you can be.

Chapter One

A NIGHT OF CHANGE

A story of dealing with change in our lives

It was a dark, moonless night. The sea was calm and flat. The reflection of the lights from my 80-foot shrimp trawler glimmered on the surface of the water like diamonds against the emerald green ocean.

The deck speakers played a song by The Doors, "Riders on the Storm". The lyrics bellowed into the darkness: "Riders on the storm, riders on the storm . . . into this house we're born . . . " Even though the sea was calm and still that night, I distinctly remember the song and its lyrics. Songs that had to do with the weather and the ocean sparked my curiosity. But this song would stay in my life forever as a reminder of how and when your life will change forever.

Think of a time when you have been faced with great change, and how it affected your life in all sorts of different ways.

Sometimes we are faced with great change in our lives. At times, the change seems cruel and unjust. At other times, the change is welcome. The bottom line is that we cannot control change and how that change will shape us into who we are. However, we do have a choice in how we interpret the change when it happens.

When I was 27 years old, something happened that would change my life forever . . .

My crew and I stared at the massive pile of Pink Shrimp on the sorting table. The problem was that there was about an equal amount of smelt, a small silvery fish, and I knew it would take hours to sort out this final catch or "tow" of the day.

I had a great crew on the boat and they were in high spirits, as we had had a phenomenal day, both catch-and weather-wise. There was a saying in the fishing industry that said, "If it was like this every day, everyone would be a fisherman." This crew had what I called "the *can-do* spirit". I attributed my success to fishing largely to the attitude and ability of men like these. They were few and far between.

We worked diligently as the murre birds amassed around the boat. They were eating the smelt as we discarded them over the side.

While we sorted, we talked about the incredible day that we had had, and what we had all witnessed at dusk. We had watched my dad and cousin load their last tow of the day. My dad's boat was much smaller than the boat that we were on. As a result, he and my cousin had to do much more work between the two of them. But that was how my dad was wired. He was a true entrepreneur and ass kicker. He had the choice of any one of his four boats to operate (or to not fish at all), but this boat was his sweetheart. My brothers, sister, and I grew up on her, tuna fishing in the summertime. The *Miss Lisa* was a friend of the family. Named after my sister, she provided for our family for much of my childhood and she was slowly edging towards retirement, as was my father.

They had such a large tow of shrimp that they were struggling to get the huge bag of the pink crustaceans to clear the railing.

The ocean was so flat that the boat was barely moving, and she was giving no assistance to the process.

We had watched in amazement as they were finally able to hoist the massive bag onto my father's boat. The cod end of the net looked like a big bluish-pink teardrop the size of a Volkswagen Beetle. As it came over the rail, it slammed into the deck boards and table with a mighty *whump*! I was proud to see my dad get such a huge catch, as he did not fish much anymore. He had always been a top producer and I had watched him build a small fishing empire over the years. I was his protégé and he had big plans for me for the future. He owned a seafood company with four very nice boats, as well as a couple of seafood restaurants in Sacramento. The possibilities were endless, and my path had been laid out in front of me. Or so it seemed at the time.

After he loaded his catch, I watched him walk into the cabin of his boat as we drifted nearby. He called me on the radio and asked me to switch to our secret radio channel. Doing as he asked, I turned on the radio but I could barely hear him in the background. We were evidently too close together for the frequency of this particular radio. I called him back on the public radio and told him that I could barely hear him, and he said some words that would stay with me for the rest of my life: *"I will tell you tomorrow."* I looked at the radio with a raised eyebrow and tried to read between the lines. I told him that I would talk to him the next day. The time was 9:30 p.m.

He was scheduled to unload his catch that night and I was scheduled to unload the next day.

I think sometimes we hear things from people around us and we let the words enter our ears, but because of the business of our lives we don't actually hear them. Although I was curious about what he had to say, I walked back on deck to join my crew in sorting our final tow.

As I walked outside, the radio was playing a Fleetwood Mac song: "Don't stop thinking about tomorrow, don't stop, it'll soon be here . . . " My crew was working diligently and the murre birds had multiplied by the hundreds. Every time a bucket of smelt would hit the water, there would be a frenzy to see who would be next at the dinner plate. It was amazing to watch the nature of it all. They would splash, squawk, and dive to get their turn.

It was approaching midnight, and it was obvious that we were going to be sorting much of the night to get this tow down below. We had a system in place—I would get some sleep while my crew finished sorting; then they would get to sleep most of the day between tows. It was usually a fair trade. I stayed for another 30 minutes or so.

Just about the time that I was heading for the cabin and my warm bunk, a murre bird swam up to the side of the boat, away from the others, and started to squawk, —no, it was different than that . . . it was more of a shrill scream. The tones, the attitude, it almost sounded like an alarm going off. It was just sitting there and sounding off, as if to tell us something. We looked at one another and started to laugh, as it was very uncharacteristic for any seabird to act this way.

I wished the crew goodnight and was off to my very warm and inviting bunk. The time was 12:30 a.m.

As I lay there, I thought about the day. The great fishing, the beautiful weather, and also the strange call from my dad. I dozed off, exhausted.

Waking from a deep sleep, I sucked in a huge gulp of air and snapped straight up, my eyes wide open. I sat there in my bunk, wondering where I was for a moment. The sound of the VHF radio was blaring in the wheelhouse. I rubbed my eyes and tried to regain my bearings. I looked at my watch and saw it was 6:30 a.m. and the sun was shining through my stateroom window. I had slept in, but that was okay today, as I knew that my crew was going to be exhausted from the night before.

Coffee was always the first priority and as I quickly got a pot brewing, I noticed the guys asleep in their bunks. I walked outside to the deck to see the progress they had made and I was pleased to see that they had completed the sorting and that the deck was spotless. It would be hard to wake them, as I knew how deeply they were sleeping.

As I walked back in, I remember all the details so clearly: the smell of the coffee that morning, the soft blue color of the ocean, and how it looked like a big shiny mirror. The gulls were squawking for their breakfast. The murre birds were gone for now, probably asleep after a hard night.

Grabbing my coffee mug, I walked up to the wheelhouse just in time to hear the tail end of a conversation between my cousins on our group radio. They sounded upset, as if something terrible had happened. I picked up the microphone, called my older cousin, and asked him what had happened. He responded by saying, "You'd better sit down." Now, I don't know about you, but when someone tells me to sit down, I have a pretty good idea that the next thing I hear is not going to be good. I instantly knew what had happened, and my heart clenched like a fist as I heard: "The *Miss Lisa* hit the rocks last night. My brother is dead and they cannot find your dad."

I sat there in disbelief. Not my dad. He was invincible. This was the kind of thing that you only hear about or see in the movies.

It seemed almost impossible, but suddenly it was like placing the final pieces of a puzzle—they just fit. I had just talked to him. *"I will tell you tomorrow . . . "*

The boat had hit the rocks on the way home at approximately 12:30 a.m. *The murre bird . . .*

I remember walking back to the crew's quarters and telling them the news. They knew my dad well and were also in total disbelief. I asked them to head the boat towards port; there would be no fishing today.

I walked into the bathroom and I remember sliding to the floor with my back to the wall as I began to cry . . .

For me, and for many of us, the experience of losing someone close to us is one of the biggest changes we will ever face. Change often comes to us when we least expect it. Life hits us with curve balls and we all react in our own way. I learned many valuable lessons from that day. I learned what it is like to lose someone that you love and admire so much. I also learned that we don't really have any control over our life's path.

There is a great saying: "If you want to make God laugh, tell him your plans."

Many of us have had our parents plan much of our future out for us—where we should go to school, what we should choose for a career, who we should marry, and so on. Coming from a four generation fishing family, I knew that I was going to have a boat someday and that I was going to follow in my dad's footsteps. Or at least that's what I believed at that time.

Looking back on that pivotal day, I also learned that many good things could come from a bad life experience. I grew up that day. I would need to be there for my mom and my family; I had just become the man of the family. I would step into a role that would thrust me into a position of carrying my dad's responsibilities and, little did I know, would be the beginning of the process of shaping my future.

Have you ever had a traumatic experience of such great impact in your life that it would change your entire being? Many people will not experience anything like this until later in life; and, although some may view that as a blessing, others that have had life-shaping experiences realize that these experiences also provide opportunities for introspection and personal growth.

I miss my dad, even though he still visits me from time to time in my dreams. Believe me, I would give everything that I have to get him back. But the experience of that night, and the days that followed, taught me a lot about myself.

They did not find my dad for another four days. It was a very sad time for my family and for our community. He was a patriarch to many. He planted the seeds of entrepreneurialism and perseverance in me. Over the years, I felt him beside me when

I spoke in front of the board of a corporation, selling them my clothing line. He was there when I started my own mortgage office. He is there when I talk to people about transforming their lives, and when I am at sea he is always with me. He was a great teacher; I look back at the short years that we had together and I realize how he shaped me into the man I am today.

Out of all of the lessons that I learned from that tragic experience, one thing really stands out as I tell this story: I am now aware that many of the things that I was feeling and dealing with were based on my beliefs, or maybe society's beliefs, of **how** I should react to the changes in my life.

I worked for the next twelve years, doing everything I could to keep my dad's dream alive. I had huge responsibilities to carry around, like anchors on my neck. I had my mother to worry about, my wife and kids, the fish company, the fleet of boats. I had more anchors than you can imagine. The funny part is that I created a lot of these anchors for myself.

My ego was in control of my vessel. As we are growing up, we are taught many things that become deeply embedded in our subconscious. We may not even know we are thinking these thoughts.

In my mind, I believed that I was supposed to carry the torch—I was supposed to be a fisherman, I was supposed to do this and I was supposed to do that. The truth of the matter was that I was trying to continue my father's story. It wasn't *my* story or *my* path. I was simply the captain of my father's vessel; it was now time to set my own course and begin to release the anchors that were dragging me down.

We all have anchors that we can work on releasing. The first step is to become aware of them.

Looking back, I now have a profound awareness of how over-whelmed I was. I was trying to be all that I could be, but within the confines of doing what I thought was expected of me. Don't get me wrong—I love the people that I was around, I love the life of the blue collar, salt-of-the-earth working man. I feel very comfortable when I am on a boat, wearing my fishing clothes. I may very well go fishing for a short period every year for the rest of my life. There was just this realization, at some point, that the fishing industry was not my path. Things had changed in so many ways. New fishing regulations, operating boats for other people, and constantly being kept away from my family caused me to realize that I was not happy. I still love to fish, but now it is a choice, not an obligation. I now know that there is so much more to life than being a character in someone else's book. I needed to follow my heart, set my own goals, and write my own book about life.

This huge change in my life helped me to realize that I needed to "see with my real eyes" . . . that I wasn't living my life for myself.

Ask yourself these questions:

- Are you living the life that you want, or are you liv-ing a life that was planned for you by someone else?

- How are the beliefs that were instilled in your mind by others affecting your decision-making process?

- What anchors are you still carrying around? What is dragging you down?

Write your answers down and really think them over. Look at them again tomorrow and see if they change as you ponder them.

My life is not perfect by any stretch of the imagination, but I have become more aware of many tools that have allowed me to release some of the anchors from my neck. I am happy, and I enjoy all of the adventures in my life. I still have anchors, and there will always be something to worry about; however, now I am acutely aware that it is my ego that will attempt to take control of my thoughts. The ego will try to take control of the helm at any chance it may have, and I cannot let that happen on my watch.

I have one more question :

- What are you doing to make a change in your routines or patterns, to create more awareness or freedom to be who you truly are inside?

I often wonder what my dad wanted to tell me that night. I wonder what the murre bird was trying to say to us. It was a night filled with many emotions and feelings, but it was also a very mysterious and magical night.

If I had to guess, I would say that my dad wanted to tell me that he loved me. He never did tell me that. The bird was probably just telling us to live every minute as if it is your last.

Life goes on and we are only here for a short time.

I learned that night that even the most experienced fisherman can run on the rocks, and that it is okay to endure these lessons in life. It has enabled me to be the captain of my own ship. Some days the seas are calm and other days they can be rough. It is just part of life.

After sitting on the floor in the bathroom for some time in total disbelief and grief, I wiped my eyes, stood up, and looked in the mirror. I knew that things would be different forever. This was a time of change. A time that would be like no other in my life. Time would continue on its own course into the future. Many other events of change would come after that night of change.

Looking back on this life-changing event in my life, I can now see how the change has become a powerful nucleus that has helped to shape my future. Life happens.

You must deal with what you can at the moment, in the best way possible. Do it in the best spirit of preparation for your future. Bring all of the light of your knowledge from your past to aid you. Do this, and you have done the best that you can do. The past is the past. No worrying or struggle can change it. It is beyond your power, as if it was a lifetime ago.

Take your past—with its sadness, weakness, and wasted opportunities—as light and confidence for the future. The situations of your past can make a difference in your present and your future. The past is the past and has gone back to where it belongs. Start with where you are in the present . . . here and now. The future belongs to you.

Chapter Two

LEADING AT THE EDGE

A story of emotional intelligence and leadership

One hundred years ago almost to the day of the writing of this book, 28 men embarked on a voyage from Great Britain to the Antarctic. On August 1st, 1914, the *MMS Endurance* left London, heading south. World War I was just getting underway and the entire expedition was in jeopardy. They were attempting to be the first expedition to achieve a transcontinental crossing of the Antarctic, from one coast to the other. The Amundsen team from Norway had just recently discovered the South Pole in 1912.

The expedition leader was Sir Ernest Shackleton. Shackleton was a man probably known more for what he failed to do, instead of what he actually achieved. He was very close to being the first to discover the South Pole in 1909 aboard the Nimrod, only to be turned around by stress of circumstances within 97 miles of the goal.

Lord Shackleton would not settle for defeat, and he assembled a team with the necessary experience to make this expedition a success. A veteran of previous Antarctic trips, Shackleton knew what it would take for men to survive against the odds.

Much of the reason that I use Shackleton as a role model for

Emotional Intelligence, (EI) is because he displayed what it is like to lead people from a place of compassion, integrity, empathy, and self-control.

As previously mentioned in this book, for many years I was the captain of several different boats. When I was younger, it was very difficult for me to be able to come from a position of positive leadership. I would get very upset and angry with people when something would go wrong. I wouldn't be held appropriately accountable and, when I look back on this time in my life, I realize that many of my actions were based on what I believed *I was supposed to do.* These actions and beliefs were based on what I had seen other people do and how I had seen them react to situations. One of the main characters in my life was my father. I learned many things from him at sea when I was a teenager. So many of his teachings about fishing stuck with me, but so did so many of his actions—both good and bad.

Why is it that we emulate those that we admire and respect? It may be a mentor or superior, it may be a coach or a friend, a sibling or other relative. We are all born with our own abilities and intelligence levels, but often we are drawn into acting and thinking like those around us, without thinking for ourselves. We must think with our hearts and minds, not our emotions.

The *Endurance* reached the Weddell Sea, just a short way from the Antarctic, on January 15th, 1915, only to be encased in ice and to become trapped. They were stuck on this ice floe for 10 months before the *Endurance* was finally crushed on October 26th by the ice and sank on November 21st, 1915, leaving them stranded.

Shackleton now had 27 men and 100 Canadian sled dogs with nowhere to stay. They were in a very dire situation and they needed to unite in their communication, their clear directive for survival, and their understanding of each others' needs.

Many times, I was also stuck in weather that was so bad that it would take every ounce of my wits to stay composed. I have a huge imagination, which is good in some situations, but at other times it allows me to create situations in my head that simply don't exist. It was when I would get into these worrisome situations that I would be engrossed in my own imaginary troubles and unable to find my leadership skills. Our life experiences will help us to get to a place where we will finally become able to make decisions based on results from our lessons in life.

As far as leading from a place of emotional intelligence, Shackleton was a master. His men respected him to the point of following him into the icy bowels of the Antarctic, knowing full well the dangers that the voyage would entail.

Here, they were in one of the most desolate places on the face of the planet. Their country was fully engulfed in a war, and there was no attention focused on them. There were no cell phones, faxes, satellite phones, or any other ways to communicate. For many people in modern times, all would have been lost. And yet, Shackleton had an uncanny way of making his men feel safe.

They would have to make some very hard decisions. First, they needed to decide what to do with the sled dogs. They simply could not continue to feed them. They were forced to put them down, and used them as part of their survival staples. This was a very difficult thing to do, as they loved these animals which brought them much comfort in their current situation. Even with a decision like this at hand, Shackleton was able to convey the facts in a way that the men would be able to understand—he was a master communicator as well.

You have to really understand the situation at hand: There were 27 men stranded, some of whom were very tough customers. They had been sailors for the better part of their lives. They did not take things lightly. Shackleton knew which people could not be with others. One of his strongest and most prominent traits was delegating to these men what they needed to do, when to do it, and who to do it with. Because of this, there was not one casualty at the hands of one of the other men.

How do you handle conflict? Are you able to delegate to others? Are you able to free up your time so you can focus on the big decisions that need to be made? Sometimes our lives and our jobs can seem so out of control and overwhelming, but our situations are actually myopic in comparison to what these men were facing.

The bottom line is that people just want to be treated with respect and dignity. They want to be heard and to have a voice. Of course, people also need to be respectful of management and follow the guidelines that were set before them. Knowing when to come from a place of compassion or empathy instead of following the company policy takes complete awareness and can take much practice on the job.

I remember having a crewman on the boat with me who was much older than I, about 15 years my senior (I remember him from when I was a young boy of about 10 years old). He had just returned from Vietnam as a soldier. He was a friend of the family and had worked for my dad before going off to the war. I remember watching him out in the field in front of our house on a Triumph motorcycle, doing insane jumps for about 20 yards through the air and landing, only to turn around and do it again, and again. It was almost as if he had a death wish.

He was not the kind of guy that you wanted to mess around with, as he would have no qualms about punching you in the nose.

We were fishing out of Newport, Oregon in the mid- 1980s and I was fairly new as a skipper. I remember coming home from Newport, completely frustrated, and talking to my dad about how this guy wasn't listening to me—when I would ask him to do something, he would sometimes disregard my instructions and start talking to another crew member about how I didn't know what I was doing. It was a tough situation for me . . . here was a guy that went to fight for our country and didn't take anything from anyone, and he was not about to listen to me!

My dad's response: "You need to talk to him like a man." That was it! Talk to him like a man? What the hell did that mean? I was 24 years old! My advice was to chew this guy out, take him back on the ocean, continue to live with him in a contained area, and hope he doesn't punch me in the nose! That would be nothing short of being in a prison cell with a murderer/rapist and telling him that you didn't like the way he looked!

I was beside myself . . . I didn't know what to do or how to handle it. So I did what any other 24-year-old would do—I fired him. That was how I dealt with it. I got rid of the problem. Looking back on that experience, I can honestly say that I would have handled things differently, knowing what I know now. He left without any objection, but could not stand to

leave without telling me exactly what he thought of me. We
have since become good friends again, and much has happened
and changed since those days.

If I were in that situation again, I may have listened to the
lesson that my father had given me. I understood now that,
when it comes to business and dealing with others in a mature
and emotionally intelligent way, I should have asked him what
he wanted from the job, or what his goals were. When asking
someone what they want, you are giving them the opportunity
to start a dialogue with you. Instead, I was coming from a place
of fear and intimidation. There was no conversation. There was
no way that he would ever have owned one of our boats; he was
just there for the job and the money. There could have been a
compromise, or we could have made a deal. I had my needs as a
new captain, and he had his needs as well. As it was, he was not
coming from a place of respect, because I was not allowing that
to happen. As it turned out, he got in his truck and drove back
home . . . end of the problem, right? Not at all. After sitting in
port, looking for a new employee, I ended up with someone
else with their own set of problems and needs.

- How do you handle a situation where you are confront-
  ed or intimidated by an employee, peer or manager or
  family member? Do you let fear intimidate you? Do
  you react in an angry way?

- What are the benefits that can be achieved by both of
  you? Can you bring up the benefits in conversation? Or
  is it easier to walk away from the challenge?

- Watching yourself can be very helpful in a situation like
  this. Be aware of how you are acting. Are you feeling
  the hair stand up on the back of your neck? Becoming
  aware of how you are feeling and reacting will give you

the opportunity to think clearly about how to respond in a logical and controlled manner. So many times we, (our ego) will react immediately without giving us a chance to respond.

Shackleton had very few options on the table. He needed to handle things in a forceful, yet diplomatic way. He created opportunities for team activities like soccer, and had the men engaging at many different levels. These men believed in him as a leader and they listened to what he told them. Their lives were in his hands. He was forceful, yet compassionate. He treated his men with respect, but demanded performance. He always had an open ear to those with a problem. He was able to fit into most groups in society, in order to make things happen. He was truly gifted in many ways.

After living in the Antarctic for almost two years from the day that they got stuck in the ice, Shackleton knew that he would have to do something extraordinary to save his men and himself. They had salvaged the three lifeboats from the *Endurance* and had literally dragged them across the Antarctic on sleds.

Once they reached Elephant Island, Shackleton ultimately provisioned one of the three lifeboats to take four of the men and sail 800 miles, back to the South Georgia Island to seek help. The other remaining men ended up building shelters out of the other two boats and survived another 4 months. Shackleton eventually returned to rescue them all. This is still one of the most unbelievable and famous nautical stories in maritime history.

What are you doing to help make your team extraordinary? Are you going to extremes to show your people that you care about them? Do you take time to listen to your subordinates, your friends and peers, and your family? We are living in very stressful times and we need to make an extraordinary effort to make a difference in others' lives.

There are many other great leaders throughout history that have exuded high levels of EI. It is such an important skill to have, that many companies are actually testing their employees to find their current management's levels of EI. These companies realize that their workforce is dealing with incredible levels of stress, and they need to address this to be able to increase productivity, or maintain high productivity. Take a look at yourself and find a place where you can test your own EI. You may be surprised where you stand. The good news is that you have your whole life to improve your EI skills, as opposed to your Intellectual Quotient, or IQ, which is usually set for life at the age of 13. Of course, you have to want to improve.

After teaching EI in over 40 cities in the U.S. and Canada, I look back at my days as a sea captain. There are many instances where I could have handled things differently. I still have moments where I get angry, sad, frustrated, and anxious. One thing I know now is that I am human and I am going to have a reaction to every situation. You can't escape that part of life. If you had no emotional reactions to different situations, you would either be hiding your emotions or fooling yourself.

I am convinced that the key is this: become aware of your emotions as they come in. Once you are aware of them, then you can acknowledge the emotions and ride it out until it calms down.

There are many other ways to deal with emotions that plague you in everyday life. I like to listen to different thought leaders on podcasts or radio programs through my headphones. I also make time to cycle or to find some form of release through cardio exercise. It is very apparent to me that if I do not use these release methods, the emotions will dangerously, and unnecessarily, fester in my life.

Many people simply choose to react in unhealthy ways to their emotions. We see this in acts of road rage, random acts of violence, kids and adults bullying one another. It isn't hard to find. We can even see this in our world leaders, and how they respond to different situations. The lack of EI may ultimately be the downfall of life as we know it. The capabilities are there to eliminate the entire human species.

We always talk about how we need to treat one another with kindness and compassion, and how we need to slow down and take the time to smell the flowers. It seems like it is getting harder and harder to do so as our lives seem to get busier and busier.

I believe that we can collectively become better at not only who we are, but *how* we are. Find that person that you admire in your life who shows actions and attitudes of kindness. Pattern your ways after them. It might be as simple as opening the door for someone or buying him or her coffee. Take an employee to lunch and ask them how things are going. Yes, it takes effort on your part.

Coming from my background, I know for a fact it is not always easy to take irrational behavior from others with a smile on your face. It isn't easy to control your emotions when things are difficult in your life. Leading by example is very important, and this is largely what got Shackleton and his men through their ordeal. They also had something else—faith. Faith in the fact that there was something much larger in their lives. We need to have faith that we can get through the hard times and that there is a reason for being alive.

I like to ask people where their thoughts come from. Many

people pray, and they believe that they get answers from a higher power based on what their belief structure is. Then, when you ask those same people if it is possible that our thoughts come from somewhere else, they will argue that point because of their beliefs.

I believe that you have to look at both as if they are coming from the same place. Most of us truly know when we are off base or treating someone wrongly. The key to improving our EI is in acknowledging this and working on correcting our behavior.

Shackleton saved his men and continued to make additional journeys to the southern hemisphere. He ended up dying at 47 years old of a massive heart attack in the South Georgia Islands, where he was buried. His men would rendezvous there and have a reunion to celebrate their leader, who they affectionately named "The Boss". This is a testimony of how people treat you, in both life and after death, when you are a compassionate and emotionally intelligent leader.

How do your friends, colleagues, and employees see you? Are you going to have people gather in your memory after you've gone? What will they think when you pass on?

In the words of a very salty old fisherman that I know, "Make sure that you quit fishing by the time that you are 70 . . . you want to make sure you can still enjoy your life." What that says to me is this: enjoy your life in every present moment, as it goes by quickly and then we are gone. You will be remembered for eternity by the legacy that you leave behind.

Chapter Three

SAILORS AT HEART

The human condition

Captain Leonid, of the Russian trawler *Ms. Taymyr*, poured another shot of vodka for the American visitors and his crew; he raised his glass in a toast to camaraderie and successful fishing. We had been invited over to the 320-foot ship for dinner and, of course, vodka. We all toasted *"Nostrovia!"* and the Americans all slammed our drinks down. The Russians, however, were more disciplined and they sipped their drinks. The reason would become apparent later as they carted the Americans back to our drifting fishing boats.

We were part of a joint fishing venture with the Soviet Union in the early 1980s. The Olympics had been boycotted by President Jimmy Carter and the relations were strained, to say the least.

I looked around the room at the different characters and I was amazed by how much these people were just like us. Many of them had asked us to find certain things for them: prescriptions for reading glasses, Levi jeans, and many other things that they could not get in the Soviet Union. They were simply getting by, and they did the best with what they had to work with. Some of these people, men and women alike, would be at sea for over 300 days a year.

The commissar was always present and it was well known that he was reporting to the KGB. He was always at the dinners and he also monitored any trading that we did between our vessels. We were interested in getting fur hats and they were interested in getting beer. It was a very fair trade. We would often see the commissar run out on the back deck and grab the case of beer off of the net after we passed it over to them.

Looking back, I often wonder what became of Capt. Leonid and the rest of his crew. Leonid had invited me and my brother to join him at his house on the coast of the Black Sea. He had two cars and two homes. He was very proud of this, as most people could not even own one car, or house, for that matter.

Since those days, we have seen the fall of the Soviet Union and the small countries around Russia form their own democracies. Many people from Russia and the surrounding countries have since moved to the United States over the last few decades.

As I am writing this book, the Russians—led by Vladimir Putin—are again seeking to create a Soviet-style union of these countries. Many people are being hurt and killed in the Ukraine, and they are required to defend their families, properties, and freedom once again. This is a cycle that repeats itself throughout history.

There is an insanity that lies at the heart of the human condition, and it can be monitored by simply researching the different wars and the acts of the respective military and political leaders. There are new signs that the Middle East is once again taking a turn for the worse, as U.S. and Israeli relations seem to be deteriorating, the war on terrorism perpetuates in Afghanistan, and other smaller skirmishes continue to pop up around the world.

The collective ego of our planet continues to thrive on having the best and the latest things. And greed, human slavery, and the polluting of rivers, cities, and oceans to get these things creates turmoil. All we need to do is watch the evening news to see that politicians are making decisions that are not necessarily in the best interest of the people that they govern. As I write this, the U.S. Congress has an approval rating of 9%—one of the lowest approval ratings in history.

Fear, greed, and the quest for power are the driving forces behind these unconscious and misguided actions of our world leaders.

The average person in any country is carrying the burden of these ego-based decisions made by their leaders, and we seem to be unable to do anything about it but sit back and watch.

In the early 1980s, at the beginning of my fishing career, I experienced something eye opening . . . something that anyone who travels abroad has also been able to witness. It is not necessarily the people of the different nations of the world that are the problem—we are all simply Sailors at Heart. It is the insanity of the leaders and their controlling propaganda that continues to fuel the behaviors that threaten the very existence of the human species.

Earlier in the day before our dinner, the fishing was hot and heavy. As the 300-foot Soviet fishing trawler *Miss Tymur* turned to starboard and pulled away, we gladly posted another impressive day's catch into the fishing logs.

Fishing on a joint venture with the Soviets was a gravy train, at times. We were catching Pacific Whiting, a fish that was present in mass quantities on the Northwest Coast of the United States. Whiting wasn't known as a delicacy, but it was used by the Soviets for fishmeal that would be turned into bread and other products to feed the motherland. Of course, there were also times when it wasn't gravy—the weather would get nasty in the summer time, we were out for long periods of time, and there was also a political element to the fishery.

The process went like this: after the U.S. catcher boat hauled in their catch, the Russian trawler would come alongside the American boat, both moving forward at the same speed, and the trawler would trail a transfer line back to the catcher boat. Once they had connected the transfer line to the catch, they would disconnect the 30-ton bag of fish and release it adrift until the Russian vessel could start hauling the bag in. The Soviets were not allowed to fish in the U.S. waters, but they could buy fish from the Americans on a joint venture and process them at sea.

As we all know, things appear to be different since the end of the Cold War . . . but different in what way? Has the Soviet Union dissolved to give way to other empirical rule, one that is covered with the illusion of democracy? And if we really want to look at the commonalities of the world, we might even see that many other countries—including the Western nations of the world—are living under an illusion called democracy when, in fact, many of the methods to elect our officials are not in the hands of the average citizen.

Today, we spend $200 for tennis shoes. We are experiencing rising prices, and the fear of hyper-inflation is looming on the horizon. Many liberties are disappearing daily as the elected officials continue to push their agendas forward in Congress and the Senate.

It seems as if the former Eastern Bloc nations of the Cold War have loosened some of the iron-fisted rules, while the Western nations continue to tighten their regulations and laws.

The human condition is one that will continue to change

throughout time. There will always be tyrannical rulers that will want to eliminate another nation. One would hope that our rulers are resilient enough to continue the surveillance of such rulers and keep them suppressed with sanctions or military force. Hitler was a fine example of a ruler consumed by with his desire to rule the world and bring great harm to others. His actions can only be described as insane. We must look closely at the fact that he was one single man with a great ability to control millions of people with his persuasive words and propaganda. What is happening right now to people around the world? Where do the answers for our human condition lie?

I often think back to Captain Leonid from the Soviet trawler and recall how friendly he was . . . how proud he was to be able to own two cars. This is something that I took for granted in the U.S., and a privilege that many others in our country also take for granted. Looking back, it seemed like our lives were very different then . . . but now they do not seem so different at all.

- What do you take for granted in your life?

- What has changed for you lately?

- What freedoms do you see slipping away?

We are again in the middle of major change in the world. Some people embrace this change, and others do not.

There seems to be a change in the way that we are viewing one another. There is more awareness of the way bullies treat other kids. There is awareness of the importance of Emotional Intelligence in some of the top corporations in the world. There is awareness in professional sports of how young, gifted athletes respond to huge amounts of cash.

We are becoming more aware of how our leaders are using the average person as a pawn in their master plan. We are noticing the power that television has to program the minds of millions, in regard to politics and religion.

There is a massive movement of people who are aware of the lack of consciousness and the collective insanity in the world. Many people go to church every weekend to be forgiven for their sins . . . and then go back to work on Monday and continue to do things in their business that many would consider a sin.

What can we do to change for the better? What can you personally do? We can continue to become aware, and help to create awareness in others. We can continue to look for that person that is hurting inside and be a beacon of hope for them.

Those who are wise advise against getting wrapped up in the materialism of the world. Yet many find it hard to keep from the Black Friday sales and the marketing that permeates their minds during the holidays—and throughout the rest of the year.

It is time that the collective people of the world begin to understand that we are in this together. We are the hope for the future. Not the leaders of the world—they are simply playing out their roles as they see fit. Their legacy is what is truly important to them.

However, we are starting to see some new faces on the scene. Pope Francis is showing that he has no interest in the opulence of the Vatican. He is reaching out to the poor of the world. The leader of Uruguay, Jose Mujica, has no interest in living in the Presidential Palace, no use for motorcades or any other frills. As a matter of fact, he has designated the palace as a homeless shelter.

These are men that are conscious of their actions. They are beacons for us to see the way. Many of us are living an abundant life, and we do little to help others. It is through giving that many will receive.

It is extremely important that we wake up to the fact that we are all in this together and that we can make a difference. But it takes the examples of great leaders like these. Will there be more? Are you one of them? I ask myself, "Am I doing enough to create a collective consciousness to make changes that improve our world?"

I often wonder about the people from the Soviet Union that I met years ago. I hope that their lives are better now because of the fall of the Soviet Union. There is still disturbing news from the Ukraine and Russia; but then again, there is plenty of disturbing news from all around the world.

We can all continue to strive for a higher level of consciousness. It takes research, open ears, and open minds. Our survival, our children's survival and our grandchildren's survival may depend on it.

We can make a change for the better because humans have the highest intelligence on the planet . . . at least when we decide to use it.

Change takes time and discipline. But, after all, we are all Sailors at Heart, equipped with the potential for greatness and the ability and knowledge to survive many storms.

Chapter Four

THE BAR CROSSING

A lesson in teamwork

As I watched the rope snap, I was sure that this was it. The jetty was so close to the boat and, as I watched the Coast Guard turning around to come back to us, I knew that we only had a matter of minutes. The swells were climbing behind us, and this was one of the most notorious bars on the western coast of the United States. I looked at my crew, busy donning their survival suits. The captain of the 44-foot Coast Guard boat came across the radio and said, "We've got you, Captain. . . hang on." That did little to calm my nerves, as I knew that they would be able to do nothing as the next set of swells came across the Humboldt Bay entrance. . .

My story goes back to 1992. We were fishing for rock cod off of Cape Mendocino in Northern California. We had weekly limits of rockfish, and sometimes we would travel 10 hours before setting our net. At the time, if you did not catch your weekly limit, you simply missed out on that portion of your monthly total. Essentially, it did not matter what the weather was like; good or bad, you simply had to go.

On this particular trip, the weather was bad. It had been raining and blowing since we left port. Winds were gusting up to

30 knots. At times, the seas were recording swells between 12 and 14 feet.

To catch the rockfish, we used a net that was towed between the surface and the bottom of the ocean. This meant we were able to fish in rougher weather, without having to worry about snagging the rocky bottom.

In this type of weather, it was imperative that the crew understood our system of setting the net, and were able to operate in unison. One mistake could spell disaster.

I had a pretty good crew on this trip. They were not great, but they were good at what they did. I had my main man, Dave, who had been with me for four years. Dave was well on his way to being captain, and he had seen many people come and go over the years. The other man, Ken, had recently joined our team. Ken was a nice guy, but very opinionated. He did his job well, but he could not seem to keep his mouth shut sometimes. It had not reached a boiling point yet, but he just could not seem to stop with his complaining.

In the fishing industry, crew selection was slim, and sometimes you had to take what was available. I had trained some good men from scratch and had seen them blossom into captains. At other times, men came and went, without really developing their full potential.

In the fishing industry, the job interview process has always been fairly informal. Word of mouth was usually enough to let us know whether crewman had issues, or what caliber of crewman they were. Later, when I started my career in the mortgage industry, I was exposed to the "Corporate America " way of doing things. Throughout my subsequent speaking and training career, I have also been interviewed many times and I am now well-rehearsed in how most people conduct an interview.

One of the topics that I speak about frequently is Emotional Intelligence, or EI. As I've already mentioned, EI is something that I take a great interest in. EI is a very powerful tool that is helping people become aware of their ability to be compassionate, self-aware, and more empathetic to others. Emotional Intelligence is used in corporate America to test employees, as well as executives, in order to determine their level of coping abilities. There are several testing companies around that actually have the final say in the outcome of the candidate. They must pass with an 80% grade on the 27-question test.

But this type of testing simply did not exist in the fishing industry. We would do the best we could do, and word of mouth was usually the best way to judge a crewman.

So, there I was with Dave and Ken out on our boat, in bad weather, looking for rockfish. On this particular trip, because it was a Friday, our strategy was to fight the weather for the next couple of days and to go into Eureka to unload. Eureka was only two hours from the place we fished, so we could go and unload on Saturday, then go back out to get our next limit and take it home. The only serious challenge was crossing the Humboldt Bay Bar in the wintertime.

After running all night and enduring the weather, we arrived at our fishing spot at about 3:00 a.m. The weather was still blowing and raining. I woke the crew up; when Ken came outside, he started cussing about the weather. He said that we should not have left port the previous night. He felt that we could have come out the next day and not had a lousy ride. Of course, he was not paying the bills and all he had invested were his rain gear and rubber fishing boots. He had to complain about everything, it seemed! Dave glanced at me and rolled his eyes.

We set the midwater net and made one pass across the rocks

where the fish live, and we got our quota of rock cod. By 4:30 in the morning, we had our load of fish put away and headed for Eureka. We would be there right at daylight and, more importantly, we would be there at the peak of the tide. Everything was going as planned . . . until the boat turned hard over to port side.

Slowing the throttle down, I ran downstairs to the engine room and I could see instantly what had happened. The steering system had a fluid reservoir on top of the steering pump, and the bolt that goes up through the reservoir had somehow sheered off. The lid to the reservoir was on the floor and the power steering fluid was everywhere. Without power steering fluid, there is no power steering. And without power steering, it was going to be near impossible to steer this eighty-foot boat across the bar at Humboldt Bay.

Our best option was for one of my crew to take a bin board from the fish hold and hold it, like a cover, on top of the reservoir all the way to Eureka! It was a two-hour run and they would have to take turns spending time in the engine room. This would be very uncomfortable, as the engines in the engine room are roaring and the heat becomes unbearable after a while. I knew my main deckhand, Dave, would be okay with this, but as you can imagine by now, Ken was going to be another story.

I asked both men to come inside so I could explain the situation. Before I could even finish, Ken said "You want us to *what*? I am not going down there for two hours!" Dave then jumped in with his can-do spirit and said that he would take the entire shift on the way to the harbor. I knew I could count on him. Ken shot Dave a nasty glance and stormed to the back deck.

Ken could not seem to control his emotions, and his attitude was starting to bleed over to Dave and me. It never fails—when someone on a boat (or in an office or business setting) starts copping an attitude, it will infect the entire operation. Looking back at this time in my life, it is almost comical to think about how much I would put up with, just to keep a crew.

As we headed towards Eureka, Ken agreed to take his turn helping after all. Dave was a good leader and taught by example. Seeing that Dave was going to do his watch either way made Ken re-examine his behavior. Ken was about 10 years his senior, and it showed me that if you have the right mindset and attitude, you can lead without any sort of title. Dave had great leadership capabilities.

As we approached the entrance to Humboldt Bay, the wind had let up, but there was still a significant swell of about 12 to 14 feet. The bar at Humboldt Bay had a reputation of being one of the riskiest bars to cross on the West Coast. A "bar" is an elevated region of sediment that occurs outside of any river or estuary entrance to a harbor. The sediment must be dredged at certain times of the year, as it will become riskier to cross in times of rough weather. You would want to time it so that you were at the entrance right before high tide. The best time to cross was when the water was still flooding into the Bay. After high tide, when the water started to ebb (flow back out), the current pushing against the ocean waves would actually cause the ocean to stand up, take an ordinary swell, and cause it to break like a wave on the beach. This could cause severe damage to a vessel, or even capsize it. It is of great concern on any given day, but even more so if you were having mechanical issues, as we were.

Upon arriving at the sea buoy just outside the entrance of Humboldt Bay, I stopped the boat and asked for both crewmen to come up on the deck. I thanked them for their hard work and I explained to them that I would need one of them downstairs to continue to secure the power steering system, and the other to go upstairs in order to convey to me what the swell was doing as I crossed the bar. Dave agreed to take the engine room detail and Ken would be upstairs. The crossing would take about 15 minutes, if all went well. Once they took their stations, I pointed the bow towards the entrance and we were off.

At the entrance to the channel there are two rock walls called jetties, one on the north side and one on the south side. They stand about 20 feet high and serve as protection from the wind and ocean swells. You want to stay as close as possible to the south jetty, in order to avoid the breakers on the north side of the channel.

The swells were on my stern (the rear end of the boat). I started my approach and, when we were no more than 100 yards past the tips of the jetties, my power steering stopped! This meant that we would continue being propelled in towards the jetties with no steering!

We were now in a terrible position. I knew that there was no way that we would be able to transit the rest of the way up the channel into safe water. The only choice was to turn around and get back out to the open sea.

As I cranked the steering wheel with all of my might, Dave immediately knew what had happened when he heard me drop the throttle and start to back up. He came running up to the wheelhouse and helped me turn the wheel. There was no sign of Ken. Once we got the boat heading west, we were faced with a set of swells coming straight at us. We plowed over the top of them, dipping the bow on the way back to safety. Eventually, Ken joined us in the wheelhouse, saying that he was getting ready to abandon ship. While I understood his concern, that would be a perilous mistake in the heart of winter. One of the most important rules of the sea: never leave the boat until absolutely necessary.

Drifting back at the sea buoy, I took a moment to calm myself, and realized that we would need to have the Coast Guard come to our aid. There are Coast Guard stations located within a few miles of every rough bar entrance in the United States. Making the call and describing our situation, they were soon on their way. They have personnel on site at these stations, so it does not take them long to get underway.

At this point in time, the Coast Guard was still using what they called their 44-foot rollover boat, affectionately called a 44. For any of you that have seen these boats train in rough bar conditions, it is something to behold. They actually strap themselves inside of these boats and cross in the worst of conditions, smashing their way out through the breakers! At times, they will be airborne and then at other times they will lay sideways and attempt to roll the boat over. They do this to train their personnel for what that would be like in a real situation. I have a huge respect for the people that have signed up for this duty!

As you can imagine, teamwork is imperative for success while engaged in a rescue. The Coast Guard training is endless for the select few that are chosen for this line of work. They all have specific duties and operate with the same standard of efficiency as any other branch of the military. Communication is key— all the way from the initial distress call, throughout the rescue mission, and then back to the slip. There is never any confusion about who is in charge. To operate a rescue any other way in these conditions would be risky.

Within 20 minutes, we made our first visual contact of the 44 as she plowed her way towards our disabled vessel.

There were times when we would complain endlessly about the Coast Guard harassing us about our safety equipment violations, but, at times like this, we felt nothing but immense gratitude for these brave people.

As the 44 approached us, I had already established radio communication with the captain. He explained their procedure to me, and I in turn conveyed it to my crew. They were standing on the bow, waiting for the Coast Guard crew to toss them the throw line, which would be attached to the actual towline.

They heaved us the line and my crew quickly threw the eye of the towline on our bow cleat. The towline is a heavy braided rope, about an inch and a half in diameter. It had an incredible breaking strength.

Once we had the line secured, we gave them the signal to go ahead. I felt the tug as the 44 began to pull us toward the entrance to Humboldt Bay. I felt an incredible weight lifted off of my shoulders. But as it turns out, the story doesn't end there. . .

The captain of the 44 told me that he was going to hug the wall of the south jetty, and that he was very concerned about the fact that the tide was now ebbing from the entrance. Time was of the essence.

I was amazed as I watched his crew operate; they performed their duties with so much proficiency. I was in awe of how good training will bring a team together.

One other important thing to remember is that the 44-footer was only half of the length of our boat. It was incredible how much power she had!

As they pulled us towards the entrance, it was obvious how much the swell had increased. The current was beginning to push against the incoming swells, causing them to appear to have peaks on them—that point just before waves break.

We continued forward and, while I completely trusted the Coast Guard Captain, I still found myself very concerned by how close we were to the jetty. It appeared as if you could jump from our boat to the rock wall. The captain assured me again that we were okay and that this was standard procedure. Regardless, it was difficult to rest assured, especially as the swells started to roll under us. At times, I lost sight of the much smaller vessel that was towing us. Looking out the back window, I could see what appeared to be about a 15- to 18-foot swell building up behind us. The 44 was about 50 yards ahead of us. As the large swell rolled underneath us, I watched the 44 disappear again. I watched as she reappeared on top of the swell and the towing rope stretched tight. I felt a pit in my stomach as I watched the line snap right before my eyes. There was a loud *zing*! The towrope was now limp and I could see the Coast Guard crew hurriedly pulling their portion of the line back on their boat.

My crew quickly ran outside and pulled our portion of the broken line back on the bow of our boat. Ken barked at me as he came in the door, "I knew this was going to happen!" I responded quickly, "Not now, Ken!" He could tell by the tone of my voice that it would not be worth saying another word, and stomped back into the galley and sat at the table.

The captain came on the radio quickly and told me that they were pulling a new line out, and to hang on. He added that they would need to let the next set of swells go through before they could approach us. I felt sick to my stomach. I looked out the door and the south jetty was right there. I looked out the back window and I could see the first wave of the next set coming towards us. The size of that first wave was nothing to worry about, and the swell was pushing us straight up the channel. I remember seeing the Coast Guard crew working as their boat was now in a hard turn, heading our way.

With my knees starting to shake I watched them turning towards us as the fifth swell passed beneath the boat with no problem, but the sixth was much sharper, as we rose to the top and slid down the backside of the swell. The seventh and final swell was coming at us and looked as if it was going to break. By now, we were laying broadside to the waves. This was not a good position to be in. The chances of rolling over when hit by swells in this direction was significant. I looked at Dave and told him to hang on as we rode up the face of this enormous swell. The 44 was standing by, helpless to do anything but wait for the outcome. The trawler tipped to what had to be 40-degree tilt and the refrigerator door flew open, emptying all of the contents on the galley floor. Ken began swearing loudly. The swell fizzled at the last second, allowing us to live for another day. The spray came off the back of the wave as it crashed along the jetty, and we tilted the other way, sliding down the back of this wall of water.

The 44 popped over the swell and was on her way towards us again. It was imperative to get this towline, as we might not get another chance. I could hear the captain on the loudspeaker, and his crew was responding systematically. They heaved the second line over to us and, once secured, they began to turn up the channel and started pulling us to safety.

The Coast Guard showed us many things that day—most significantly their teamwork. They were well-trained and totally prepared, so there was no confusion and no stress with the mechanics of their procedures. They showed patience and professionalism. They communicated clearly amongst themselves and with us. We knew exactly what each member of their team was doing and planning at all times. It really showed me that I was lacking in many areas, and highlighted how I could improve the operations on my boat, especially with some of the recent incidents.

As soon as they finished cleaning the mess from the untimely opening of the refrigerator, I asked Ken to join me in the wheelhouse. Even as we were being towed up the channel, I explained to him that there was no room for anyone on my boat to act the way he acted and that I did not appreciate his behavior. I told him that I want a crew of team players that are behind me 100%. I gave him the option to stay on as part of my crew and work to improve his behavior, or he could choose to leave. He chose the latter, something that did not surprise me. I knew that this was going to be best for both of us. Ken lacked emotional intelligence. Had he had insight, he would have offered create solutions to the problems we had rather than curse and act like a victim.

Once we were safely to the mooring, I was glad to personally meet the crew of the 44. These men showed much bravery that day and I was honored to shake their hands.

They were an example of solid teamwork, communication, and emotional intelligence. There was no panic, despite the rapidly changing conditions and inherent risk in what they do. They were confident that their training would help them achieve success.

Leadership and solid communication are a big part of any team. Companies and organizations are realizing that the level of emotional intelligence of their players is so important. The Coast Guard captain showed impeccable leadership skills by staying calm and being in control of his men. Controlled behaviors in tense situations will produce positive and efficient results. This is a great example of how becoming more emotionally intelligent can help produce successful results within any organization.

Have you tested your team's level of emotional intelligence?

Many corporations such as Mercedes Benz, Toyota, and Estée Lauder are now testing their employees' and executives' levels of emotional intelligence (EI) prior to hiring them. The marketplace is changing, and the way we get along with one another is becoming increasingly important. Everyone struggles with challenges, both on and off the job. But often, people keep those struggles to themselves until they get to the point where they are overwhelmed. Assessing their emotional intelligence will give employers a baseline indication of their employees' ability to balance life's challenges, put things in perspective, and work through issues. This is where the testing of EI is so valuable to any company or organization.

On a scale of 1 to 10, what is your level of emotional intelligence? Are you listening to your employees or peers? Are you being empathetic to their needs?

I recently watched the movie *Mutiny on the Bounty*. If you have never seen this movie, the captain of the *Bounty*, Captain Bligh, was anything but emotionally intelligent. He had a very hardline way of doing things. It is no wonder the crew mutinied, based on the way he treated them. His first mate, on the other hand (Fletcher Christian, played by Marlon Brando), was compassionate and understanding of what the crew was dealing with and feeling. He was able to get things done without overreacting emotionally.

The captain of the 44 was clearly in charge of his men—he wasn't just their boss, he was their leader. This is something that is earned based on actions. When we met on the mooring, there was an obvious sense of respect from his crew.

Do you have the ability to lead your people and gain their respect? Do your subordinates lead with the proper skills that will gain the respect of their team?

So, what did I learn that day on the bar? I learned some basic facts about teams:

- Any team has a chance to succeed at the beginning of any venture.

- Interviewing properly is mandatory, because a great team starts with the right people, selected for the right reasons.

- Having a person with a bad attitude in the group is never beneficial.

- Emotional Intelligence is something that is critical and is being used to test executives and employees.

We need the following components in place to have a solid team:

- Leadership (Are you being a great leader, or do you have the proper leader in place?)

- Communication (Are you communicating well with your team? Are you listening to your team?)

- Preparation (Are you interviewing well? Are you thoroughly selecting talent based on their ability or are you hiring people emotionally?)

- Training (How often are you training your team? Are they getting the most modern and state-of-the-art training?)

If any of these components are not in place, the odds of success will vary. A poorly-built team could succeed against all odds. But for reliable, repetitive success, a strong team is vital.

Remember, sometimes the first place to start to examine your team is to look at yourself. The fact that you are reading this today shows that you have the vision to lead and that you want to improve your ability to lead your team.

Teamwork is not always going to result in a life or death situation, such as my story, but when you are in a situation as intense as I was, you tend to see all of the good and bad aspects of your team. The way the captain handled his crew and operation, and the seamless interaction of all the men on the 44, helped me to see how I could improve. The way that Ken was acting was unacceptable and needed to be dealt with immediately.

As a leader, I encourage you to ask yourself these questions:

- Are you at the top of your game? Are you leading with an open ear? Are you leading with emotional persuasion?

- Do you have any people like Ken on your team?

- How long have they been there? How long is it going to continue?

It is up to you to be the example for others. You are a leader. Lead with compassion, communication, and conviction to be the best that you can be.

Chapter Five

THE STRANGEST STORM

Weighing out risk-based decisions

Most of us have, at one time or another, been faced with risk-based decisions. These are those decisions that require you to act quickly, to decide on a course of action with little time to ponder the implications

As a commercial fisherman, you can probably easily imagine that I have been faced with many situations and decisions like these, which were not only risk-based but also possibly a matter of life and death. And at times, those same decisions did not only affect my own life, but potentially risked the lives of my crew as well.

After the death of my father in 1987, I set out to do my part to save his business and keep his legacy alive, while still taking care of my mother, my wife, and kids.

I started to fish with a vengeance. We spent 266 days—actual fishing days—on the ocean in 1988. There were many days in addition to those days that were spent either working on the fishing gear or the boat itself. This went on for many years.

I remember how, when we were docked, people would comment about how concerned they were for me and my crew, as we would be the only boat out on the water while it was storming.

I was married back then, and I remember lying in bed one night with my wife, and the wind was blowing so hard that I thought the windows were going to blow out. She looked at me and said, "Sometimes it is worse than this while you are out fishing." That really put it into perspective for me.

But still, it was a very ego-driven way of thinking. It made me proud to know that I was doing everything that I had learned from my dad, who used to say things like "Stick and stay and make her pay," or "You need to have staying power." I used to listen to these words of advice and I knew that they would make me a top producer.

I was still trying to make my father proud, even after he was dead! That is really messed up . . . talk about misplaced beliefs!

What people did not know is that we had a system in place to deal with the rough weather. My boat at the time was 80 feet long with a great set of poles, or outriggers, that had stabilizers on the end of each pole.

If you've seen the movie *The Perfect Storm* you may remember the scene when Billy Tyne (played by George Clooney), the captain of the 65-foot *Andrea Gail*, actually climbed out to the end of the outrigger in hurricane-force winds with a blowtorch. He went out to cut off the plate of steel that was swinging around. That, ladies and gents, was a stabilizer.

They were placed below the water in rough weather to control the roll of the boat. Evidently, in this movie, it was way too rough and they were coming out of the water, causing mayhem and destruction to the boat.

We would put our stabilizers into the water and then we would idle into the oncoming storm. We would weather it out for sometimes for two or three days at a time. We would watch the weather charts; I got very good at predicting just how long it would take for the front to go through, and what size of seas, ocean swells, and wind velocity were going to be involved.

The faster the storm was moving, the sooner it would move through and we could get back to fishing.

Once again, it was my crew that made the difference in this type of weather. I had a great crew and, had I not had this caliber of crewmen on the boat, I would have thought twice about staying at sea in this type of weather. This particular crew would actually encourage me to stay and keep fishing! We were a well-oiled machine, and we worked well together. My crewmen went on to be outstanding captains in their own right.

The boat was also very safe; it was a priority to have all of the safety gear up to date, and we held safety drills on a regular basis. In light of what had happened to my father the previous year, I was very conscious about having the safety gear up to snuff.

When making risk-based decisions at this level (or any level, really), it is very important to have a strong team that knows their responsibilities and duties. I am sure this is the same in any industry.

How well is your team trained? Do you feel as if you can go into any situation against your competition and come out victorious? Or is your team going to crack under pressure at a critical moment? We had great confidence, a great team, and a safe and solid platform underneath us. We had the ability to stick and stay!

In early January of 1988, we were provisioning the boat to make a four-day trip between storms. We were leaving on Tuesday, and there was a front that was expected to come through on the weekend. Things were going well, and we were excited to get back on the water.

We were on our game and doing great. We were on course to be the top-producing boat, not only in our hometown, but the entire West Coast of the United States. This was great money and great for the ego; after all, who doesn't want to be number one?

Once we were on the fishing grounds, we settled into our routines. By the end of the second day, we were on our way to another record-breaking trip. The weather was beautiful and the fishing was fantastic! One more day and we would have the biggest load ever to be delivered by any boat in our homeport!

There was one little thing that I did not plan for, and that is the ability of Mother Nature to change her mind and throw a curve ball. . .

I remember walking into the wheelhouse and seeing the weather fax printing out an emergency weather report. This was rare, so I stopped what I was doing to see what it was about. Evidently the front that we thought was going to arrive on Saturday was moving much faster than we had originally thought, and it had also intensified!

I was now in the position of making a risk-based decision. I instinctively knew that this storm was going to be different. I knew that I was five hours from the harbor and I could easily make it in before the storm hit. However, my ego seemed to want to "stick and stay".

I talked to the crew and they felt comfortable with staying

where we were as well. I thought to myself, *This is perfect! These are two guys who are never scared of anything!*

So we stayed.

We finished the day out. It was Thursday evening. The storm was expected to reach us by 7:00 a.m. on Friday morning. We had a huge meal and turned in for a solid night's sleep. We would fish the next morning, weather permitting.

I woke up at daylight and the wind was already starting to gust up to 25 knots. The sea was building quickly, and I remember being amazed at how quickly this front was moving. I went back inside and woke the crew. We decided that it wouldn't be a good idea to set the fishing gear.

We went into the standard protocol of pointing the bow into the weather and releasing the stabilizers to do their task of keeping us comfortable.

Within two hours, the wind was gusting up to 50 knots with steady 30-knot sustained winds. This was going to be a very different storm, indeed.

I sat in my captain's chair and took the first watch as my crew slept in their bunks. There was an incredible sea building, and I sat there thinking to myself how nice it would be to be sitting in my recliner at home instead of in the jaws of what appeared to be a small hurricane.

The winds were now reaching peak gusts of 70 knots and the seas were turning into small mountains. The swells were coming from the northwest at about 20 feet now and the sea was still coming from the south. It was like being in a washing machine! Never in my fishing career had I seen a storm build this quickly.

I had a sinking gut feeling that we were in over our head, and panic was starting to set in. I was beginning to wonder if I had made a critical error and that maybe I should rethink my decision to stay.

It was definitely time to get closer to land . . . and soon.

I printed a new weather chart and it appeared that we were close to the middle of the system. There was something different about this chart, compared to the previous chart. It was still showing the rough sea heights of 20 feet, but now it was also showing northerly winds on the back side of the system that were in excess of 50 knots!

This is very uncharacteristic as, normally, a storm will slowly die down and the conditions will become manageable.

The south winds that we had been experiencing were dying down and the leftover sea was still peaking at about 15 to 16 feet.

By now, my crew was in the wheelhouse with me, as they could no longer stay in their bunks. They looked very concerned and they, too, were wishing that they were somewhere else right about now.

I was on a course for our homeport and we could literally see the wind start to shift around to westerly, and then northwesterly. It was a phenomenal, yet scary experience to see nature flex its muscle this way. This wasn't going to be good.

Have you ever been in a situation where you knew something was coming—and that it was going to be painful? You knew that, no matter what you were entering a storm and it was because you made a decision that was based on ego-driven thinking? Making a decision based only on the potential benefits to you? Taking a chance and making a critical risk-based decision where you knew that there was the possibility of an adverse outcome that could affect you, or those around you?

Maybe it was a relationship decision, or a confrontation. Maybe it was a business decision. Perhaps it was something that you regret because you didn't put enough time into your thought process?

Once we make these types of decisions, we have to "ride the wave," so to speak. We often grow from these types of experiences.

The wind was now blowing completely from the northerly direction and was right on our stern quarter. The boat handled well with a following sea, but the problem was that the sea was still coming from the south. The wind had simply not waited for the ocean to turn and join her from the other direction. This was all happening very fast now!

The wind and swell continued from the northerly direction and, because the current was still out of the south, it was causing the swell to stand up and create rogue waves.

I had heard of this phenomenon, but I had never experienced anything like this—and I have never seen anything like it since.

All of a sudden, a ferocious wave came up from behind the boat and, as I looked out of the back window, I saw a massive wall of water bearing down on us.

My knees actually started to shake as I felt the stern of my eighty-ton vessel start to rise. We were actually surfing down the front of this monster! The boat was doing her best to keep straight, but we were literally falling down the front of this wave.

This roller coaster ride went on for another 25 or 30 minutes. I was steering the boat manually, because the automatic pilot could no longer keep up with the weather.

I felt completely out of control. I was worried about my crew and worried about never seeing my family again. It was a terrible feeling. I vowed never to let this happen again. I would never put my crew into this situation again and I vowed to never let them talk me into staying. Since that day, I have maintained a tremendous respect for the ocean and the power that it can unleash.

The ego is a funny thing. We are taught and encouraged by our culture to strive for success, to be number one. I have been accused of having a gambler's spirit, taking chances against the odds to score big. I suppose that comes with the territory when you are an entrepreneur. But, taken too far, it can cause great harm.

What decisions have you made in your life that were risky? How did your ego play a role in those decisions or thoughts?

Risk-based decisions are very powerful. They have the ability to pay off in silver dollars, or the potential to cause financial ruin. You must think your decision through carefully and take into full consideration the potential ramifications you may face.

If (or when) you reach a point where there is no turning back, when you are in a place where you are totally out of control, this is a helpful technique: imagine that you can actually time travel. Allow yourself to envision where you would like to be in 5 years. Once you are in this place, look back to your current situation. Did you act with common sense? Or were you operating from a place of ego-driven thinking?

By looking ahead into the future, it will give you a better perspective of your current situation. Ask yourself these questions about your future vision:

- Are you proud of your*self?*

- Are you operating from a place of ego-driven thinking?

- Are you creating awareness of how you are making your risk-based decisions?

- Are you looking back with regrets, or are you learning from your pivotal decisions?

Then, once the decision is made, commit fully. Know that the decision that you made is done. You can't go back and change it. There is not much that you can do about it. Own it, learn from it. Even if things didn't work out, never regret having taken the chance.

We survived that day at sea, but I will always remember the way that I felt and how I narrowly avoided a possible tragedy. I began to slow down after that, and was still quite successful as a commercial fisherman. The good news is that I am here to tell these stories and share my experiences with others. I have made many decisions since that time, and there are going to be many more to come . . . but those are stories for another day.

Our success in life, or business, should not hinge on any cost to others, whether they are your employees, your family, or anyone else. We should never put our agendas or priorities over their well-being.

William George Jordan made a powerful statement about how our decisions should affect others:

"Today no one in the world shall suffer because I live. I will be kind, considerate, and careful in thought and speech and act.

I will seek to discover the element that weakens me as a power in the world, and that keeps me from living to the fullest of my possibility. That weakness I will master today. I will conquer it at any cost."

We are all human, and we all have the ability to succeed in life and also to fail. It is how we handle ourselves as we move forward that will be the mark of our legacy, how we are remembered at the end of the day.

Chapter Six

THE PIRATE WITHIN

Finding your inner leader

It was dark and rainy night in 1975. The wind was blowing 40 knots and the rain was flying sideways. The captain of the 60-foot crab boat backed up to the unloading dock. There was no one around on this stormy night. The crewman on the back of the boat took a big drag on his cigarette, and smoke billowed up around his face. He threw a heavy tie-up line to another crewmate who was standing on the dock. A third crewmember in dark green rain gear had already climbed up on top of the hoist, which was a large, A-framed boom that would swing out over the fishing boats, used for unloading crab and fish. He was waiting for the rope to be tossed to him. Once he had the rope in hand, he tied it to the frame of the hoist and quickly shimmied down to the dock. The other man yelled to the captain of the crab boat, who was standing on the flying bridge with a hand on the throttle and another on the steering wheel.

Hearing the yell, the captain shifted the boat in gear, easing forward as the line became tight on the unloading boom. Both of the crew members on the dock ran back quickly to the waiting pickup truck and backed away from the hoist. The windshield wipers were barely able to keep up with the rain as they beat back and forth. The men watched with anticipation as the rope became increasingly tighter.

They both began to grin as they watched a big plume of smoke roll out of the stack of the crab boat as the captain slammed the throttle to full speed.

The hoist came flying from the dock and made a huge splash behind the boat. The captain turned the boat towards the entrance of the harbor, dragging the hoist behind the crab boat. The pre-orchestrated plan was to pull the hoist down, drag it to sea outside of the harbor and, once they reached the deeper water outside of the harbor, cut it loose.

The men in the truck watched in amazement as the hoist flew from the dock. The driver stomped on the gas pedal of the truck, throwing gravel against the dock shack, and disappeared into the night.

The dock was now silent once again, minus a fish hoist. The wind continued to howl as the storm intensified. This was crab season in December. The weather was harsh in the Pacific Northwest this time of year, and so were the emotions of the crab fisherman. Prices were always a problem and there were strikes and price disputes every year. There were associations formed to negotiate with the crab buyers, but their efforts were usually futile. Many times, the fisherman would sit in the harbor for several months, only to get a dime per pound more for the Dungeness crab.

Many of the fishermen would try to create side markets and use their business minds and ambitions to find a way to market the crabs on their own. Some of these men would sell the product for less money than the asking price of the association. They were considered rogues and they were labeled "scabs". This angered some of the other fishermen and they would take matters into their own hands.

On this stormy night, one of the hoists used to unload the rogue crab boats was now being dragged to its final resting place. This was just another event in the string of many. Some of the so-called scab boats had been tampered with over the last month. One fisherman had his own deck hose stuck into his engine room, sinking the boat at the dock. Another boat had several bags of sugar dumped into its fuel tanks. There were threats on people's lives and tension was running wild.

My father was an entrepreneurial man and he, too, had created his own markets. It was an exciting time for our family as we were helping him to build his business. He was a hard-working fisherman and he was never one to settle. He was extremely bothered by the fact that he was on a poundage limit that was the same as some of the part-time fisherman who had other jobs, such as teaching, construction, etc. I remember him telling me that this was his full-time job and he wanted to grow his business.

My dad grew up in Wisconsin with his four brothers and two sisters. My grandfather was a lake fisherman on Lake Superior and the boys were all taught to fish. Not only did they fish, but they would also smoke the lake trout and sell them in Superior, Wisconsin. They had a process in place.: they would have fish in the smoker, fish in the brine, and they would catch more fish and rotate them out of the smoker and drive them to market.

My dad did very much that same process with the Dungeness crab. He had developed a very strong market for live crab in San Francisco, and the Bay Area in general. The fishermen would go to San Francisco almost every year, as the season there would open two weeks prior to the Northern season opener. The truth is, in those days there was probably more partying going on than crabbing. My dad told me that when they would go out to the different bars and restaurants around the wharf, he would make a point to meet the owner of the restaurants to create a relationship and get their business cards. He was smart that way.

After seeing that the market he built was taking off, he placed two cookers in his gear shed and started his business. I still remember vividly driving crab to San Francisco and making the deliveries with the other crew members, some nights sitting in the gear shed with my high school friends, scrubbing crabs and putting rubber bands on their legs. It was a very dynamic time as the crab crop was phenomenal. My father continued to build this business over the next decade and ultimately employed over 150 employees. He started two seafood restaurants in Sacramento to generate a place to sell more products. He had four boats, a seafood plant, and a small fleet of semi trucks. This all happened over a ten-year period! My dad was a veteran of the Korean war and he never finished high school. He knew how to succeed and was a pure capitalist at heart. But there was a price to his success.

He was also threatened and accused of selling crabs cheaply. I fished with him after I graduated high school. We came in and saw his truck had been tampered with. One day, the headlights were both knocked out and the glass was lying on the sidewalk. I remember the look on his face as he shook his head. He said, "There is nothing worse than someone kicking your dog because they are mad at you." That saying has stuck in my mind over the years. He always welcomed the other fishermen to look at his books; and he was happy to show them the fish and game tickets. That didn't matter to them, as they would come up with another story about how he was like the rest.

There were people selling cheap product, that was a fact. I will defend my dad, as he was an honest man and I am still very proud of him for what he accomplished.

What was most amazing to me was that he never let these actions and accusations derail him from his goal of growing his business. We would go into the local restaurant where the other fishermen would be eating lunch. Many of them would look the other way and not acknowledge his presence. He would sit down and have his lunch like it was any other day. Very interesting indeed . . . my dad had grit!

You may wonder why I called this chapter, "The Pirate Within". What causes people to get angry at others? Why does jealousy and greed cause us to be vindictive or nasty?

Many of these other fishermen were good people; and they were friends with my dad at one time or another. They had good families and their kids were friends of mine. Their wives were friends of my mother. They were not the type of people that would do anything to hurt another person.

But there were others. They were people that had a knack for nastiness and ugliness. They were masters at controlling others through intimidation. They would never be happy—no matter what. As I learned throughout my life, that it is not just ugliness in the fishing industry. There are people like that everywhere.

Business in general can be very cutthroat and intimidating. Many people will give up on their dreams and on their success because they don't want to deal with these types of people.

Corporate America consists of a hierarchal structure that will keep many people in a place of stagnation, as they will opt for the safe road in order to avoid these people.

Think about your life right now. Are you dealing with someone who is difficult? Someone who enjoys terrorizing people? These are bullies, that would get away with murder, often they are in a place of management—and maybe they are even the CEO of the company!

A pirate can be in anyone. This pirate has its own timeless intelligence. It feeds on drama and thrives on negativity. Have you ever done something that you regret; something that you would go back in time and change, if you could? Everyone has things happen in their lives that they can't control. They may not even be aware of how that pirate within got there.

The pirate can show up in many forms: sadness, fear, anxiety, worry, and the list goes on. It is an entity made up of emotion. The pirate can talk to you and convince you that you will never make it. Maybe the pirate will tell you that you need something, or you deserve something when you can't afford it. The pirate will tell you that you deserve more love, or that you are better than others.

The pirate can be dormant inside of your for years. Eventually it will need to get some fresh air and that pirate will rear its ugly head. Ladies, there were many female pirates throughout history too. The pirate is what feeds the ego. It will also feed on your thoughts. All it takes is one situation, one different experience and the pirate can be awakened.

Sometimes the situation can be minor, but that is all it takes to trigger the pirate into action. Once awakened, it will not want to be alone. It will seek to awaken other pirates until there is nothing short of a war inside. It is the pirate way . . .

Many years after my dad died, I was witness to another situation in the fishing industry where I could actually see the pirates rise out of some fishermen and generate a riot. We had been tied up for over three weeks over a price dispute. There was a report that there was a boat from a Northern port that had infringed on the price strike and dumped their crab pots

off of our port. This was crazy on his part, because you could
lose your crab pots very easily to a sharp knife.

A meeting was called and all of the fishermen met in the park-
ing lot of the harbor. The air was thick, the dynamic was intense and I remember how a couple of people were able to
anger and excite the entire crowd into action. It was like I was
watching an episode of *Gunsmoke* and they were going to lynch
someone! I was not immune to this emotional fervor. It was
agreed that something needed to be done about this guy.

I chose to go to the boat and started her up while waiting for
my crew. A couple of other guys were going with me as well.
By the time the crew got to the boat, I watched in amazement
as the boats were pouring out of the harbor. We were one of
the last boats to leave, and by the time we got to the area where
the pots were, we saw nothing but floating buoys that were
not attached to anything. I still remember hearing the captain
of the rogue boat screaming on the radio for the fishermen to
stop cutting the buoys off of his crab pots. For him, it was too
late. The pirates were attacking! It was an amazing display of
human nature and pirates had risen to do battle that day.

We all have our situations to deal with, such as when we are
in traffic on our commute and someone experiences road rage,
or when a transaction is going great and then suddenly goes
sideways, when we lose our home to foreclosure, lose a loved
one, through death or divorce. Our lives are always in a state
of flux. We must keep that pirate from attacking.

Sometimes however, it is not bad to have a pirate inside. Sometimes we need to stand up for virtue. Sometimes we need to
be an advocate for change. Sometimes we need to lead others.
Pirates are not always bad. Sometimes they can help the less
fortunate. In the words of Johnny Depp, "Life's pretty good,

and why wouldn't it be? I'm a pirate, after all."

We all have moments of negativity, when things go wrong. It is how you respond to the situations that make the difference in the outcome. Once the Critical Pirate takes over your thinking, it can be almost impossible to stop the negativity. The voice might start in your head and continue to tell you things like "you will never make it," or "you don't deserve it." "You're not good enough, who do you think you are kidding?" Over time you may even agree with the critical pirate, and identify with what the pirate is telling you. Many people will choose to stay in this mode of operation. . . STOP listening to that bad pirate! You have a choice in what you say to yourself, and act upon. You do have a choice.

You must become aware that the pirate exists inside so you can begin to control it. You may never completely control it, but you can see and feel when the pirate comes to visit.

Picture yourself standing in the kitchen, doing dishes. You hear a knock on the back door and, when you look out the window, you see the pirate standing outside. The pirate waves and points to the doorknob, wanting to come in. You smile and shake your head, No. And you go back to doing the dishes.

It is impossible not to have emotions. If you felt nothing, you would be a vegetable. You would be unable to feel happiness, excitement, or joy. The key is to acknowledge the emotion and admit that you are feeling it and identify it. *I am sad. I am worried. I am anxious. I am angry.* Feel the emotion.. Let it in for a minute if you want to, and experience it for a minute, and tell the pirate to go. Get centered.

It is very important to have faith in something. Many people have given up on their spirituality or faith in the fact that there is something much bigger than them, called a Higher Power.

Often people feel all alone. When they do this, it leaves them with no choice other than to accept that this is all that there is.

Can it be possible that we exist for 75 to 90 years on this planet, and that is all there is? I simply cannot buy that. In my opinion, there is something so much bigger in the grand scheme of things. Look into the stars and imagine that there is something bigger beyond what you can physically see. How can it be possible that this little blue sphere we call Earth is the only form of intelligence and life in something so immense? There is nothing that I enjoy more while at sea than to turn all of the lights off at nighttime and look at the stars on a clear night. There is no light source to block the beauty. I am sure any sailor would agree that there is nothing quite as beautiful.

The more you practice this awareness technique and pay attention to your emotions, the more you will begin to notice other little things in life too. You will slow down and notice the smile of a baby; the simplicity and unconditional love of a dog wagging its tail, looking for a pat on the head. You will see the beauty of a beautiful sunrise or sunset. You can look at the Milky Way and know that there is something so timeless and beautiful about life that we cannot be alone on this planet.

We are all challenged and bombarded with many problems on a daily basis, such as the economy, the environment, world disasters, and politics. The media is progressively pummeling the minds of the average person and shaping us into a land of consumers and users; instead of a world of creators and entrepreneurs. I challenge you to become aware of what is important in your life, to stop paying attention to what is useless and void of improving the lives of those around us.

There are many people looking for leaders, especially our young people. We have an increasing void in leadership in this country, as well as the world. Far too many potential leaders are taking the easy way out. Will you stand up and lead? Will you support good leaders?

For many, the level of stress in their lives is increasing by the minute. We are forced to do whatever is necessary to bend and shape, as taxes keep rising, and more laws and regulations make it harder to survive and operate our businesses.

We need to become aware of the things that are truly important to us. When the pirate starts to tell us that we are doomed, we can tell him or her calmly, "No! It is you Pirate, who is doomed to an eternity of bondage and service to do good works." Stop letting the voices behind your mind chatter control your next decision. There are many people with the ambition and the will to succeed in business, or with any other great and noble venture. The following quote by Theodore Roosevelt depicts brilliantly what I am talking about:

> "Far better is it to dare mighty things, to win glorious triumphs, even though checkered by failure . . . than to rank with those poor spirits who neither enjoy nor suffer much, because they live in a gray twilight that knows not victory nor defeat."

We all have dreams and greatness within us. We need to look deep inside and ask the question, *am I listening to the voice of malcontent in my mind? Am I listening to the naysayers that would keep me in a place of complacency for the rest of my life?* Are you pushing people away because of your anger outbursts or your actions? Are you stepping on people to get to where you want to be?

Living a life of fullness involves being compassionate to others and being self-aware of your actions and reactions.

Take a minute today to think of a time when you stopped to say thank you to your friends, family, peers, or employees. When is the last time that you complimented them on the work they did, or how they treated you with kindness?

When I left the ocean for a land job in 1999, I soon became aware of the similarities between the job on the beach and the maritime world. There is no perfect situation, and the stronger people seem to always have the upper hand and get what they wanted in life. This strength can show in different forms. It can show up in the form of intimidation like I pointed out earlier. It can also be when we control the pirate and keep him/her from entering our thoughts and we maintain a steady course towards our dreams and goals.

My mother used to say, "you can get more flies with honey than vinegar." I love that advice. She was a remarkable woman. She taught me that it takes a man to walk away from a fight. This is unconventional thinking in the fishing industry, especially if you believe you need to defend your honor in front of your peers. It takes full awareness and effort to control of your emotions.

It was my hope when I started writing this book that I might open your eyes to the experiences I've had, and that you could use my insight though my sea stories from the past decade to take you to a place you have not been before. Most of these stories are from my past life, and things are different for me now. I have experienced a lot, and this has changed the way I see things now.

I find it easier to accept things for what they are. I don't always like the circumstances, but I accept them easier. They have helped me to grow and to become a better person. I miss the ocean, and I have been lucky to go back and fish alongside my friends. I have been joined by my son and my nephew during the last few years.

I have a very deep appreciation for the sea and the beauty it brings. The beauty of the sea is not the only attraction to me. It is in my blood and always will be in my blood. I miss the sea mammals and the birds. The sunrises and the sunsets. The harvesting of the fish. The storms. The people who make their living there, and the serenity of getting away from the craziness of life on land. But most of all, I remember and miss the experiences that have shaped me into who I am today, bringing me wisdom from the sea.

I often think about the days of old, the days when there were no limits on what you could catch, the excitement of fishing with the Russians, watching my dad build his company. The stories are endless and the characters are irreplaceable. There never is a dull moment at sea.

My pirate is still inside; he talks to me from time to time. We have created a truce, a silent agreement about how to approach the future. He seems to have become more of a father to me, reminding me of what I am supposed to be doing next. He encourages me now, as opposed to when he would hold me back with negative thoughts and comments. I have a confidence now that I did not have in the past, and a knowingness that all is well and great things are rolling my way.

What is your inner voice saying to you? Are you in agreement with it? Or is it beating you down?

Look closely at your thoughts and your beliefs. Pay attention to why you think what you think. Be aware of your emotions before you react. Once words escape your mouth, there is no way you can take them back.

Tell the pirate to take a break; to be calm. Choose your battles carefully, for there is only so much time in the day. Make every minute count and live your life in acceptance of "what is," not "what if."

I remember a saying that goes like this: "You know you have mastered your life when you live a life of acceptance knowing that you have done your best."

In conclusion, I would like to leave you with a couple of quotes from some of my favorite authors; the first by William George Jordan from, *The Majesty of Calmness*:

> "I will do each day, in every moment, the best I can by the light I have; I will ever seek more light, more perfect illumination of truth, and ever live as best I can in harmony with the truth as I see it. If failure comes I will meet it bravely; if my pathway then lie in the shadow of trial, sorrow and suffering, I shall have the restful peace and the calm strength of one who has done his best, who can look back upon the past with no regret, and who has heroic courage in facing the results, whatever they may be, knowing that he could make them different."

Read this quote on a daily basis for a while and teach the pirate within that it is okay to be who you are. But don't waste a moment of pursuing your dreams, for life is fleeting and will pass you by.

The second quote, from Mark Twain, uses the metaphors from the sea and seems to be an appropriate way to end this book.

"In 20 years from now you will be more disappointed in the things that you didn't do, than the things that you did do.

So throw the bowlines from the dock, let the trade winds fill your sail, and sail away from safe harbor.

Dare to explore, discover, and dream."

So I bid you farewell for now, and until we meet again . .

Command the Pirate within to guide you along, through channels and passages, treacherous as they may be. Do not let him deceive you with his words and trickery;

For all of the years that have come and gone, knowing that your best has been done. We are who we are, so be the best you can be, live your life to the fullest, seeking wisdom from the sea.

The Captain

May You Have Fair Winds and Full Sails.

REFERENCES FOR THE READER

Pg. ix: Jordan, William George; 1898 *The Majesty of Calmness* New York: Curtis Publishing Company

Page 52: Jordan, William George; 1898 *The Majesty of Calmness* New York: Curtis Publishing Company

Page 60: Johnny Depp; Brainy Quote

Pg. 63: Roosevelt, T. Brainy Quote

Pg. 66: Jordan, William George; 1898 *The Majesty of Calmness* New York: Curtis Publishing Company

Pg. 67: Twain, M.; Brainy Quote

Made in the USA
San Bernardino, CA
23 September 2014